What Can Social Media Do For YOUR Business?

By Roberta Alluzio

ISBN:10:1537568205
ISBN-13:978-1537568201

Forward

Social Media is effective if you have a plan, a strategy for making the most of the multitude of social media platforms we have to choose from. Social Media Marketing can increase your sales, bring in new customers and build up your brand.

The question is with so many ways to turn, how should you start? This book will answer your questions about starting a social media-marketing plan. We will walk through how to plan a social media strategy, define goals, and manage your sites to developing landing pages and how to choose the right social media platforms for your business.

Let's start!

Table of Contents

Before we talk about the more popular social media platforms, let's talk about social media strategy.

Where do you start?

SECTION 1 – BUILDING A SOCIAL MEDIA PROFILE

Building A Target Audience Profile

It is crucial in order to be successful on social media to know who your target audience is. You need to know where your audience is spending their time on social media. Those are the platforms your business needs to be on. How do you find your target audience?

Using some inbound marketing strategies, you can find out what kind of social media marketing you should be doing. A good place to start is by creating an actual persona of your perfect customer. Go all the way; give your persona a name and a back-story. This will help you envision where, when and how they shop. In creating this persona, they obviously could use your product or service but what else are they interested in? Let's try it –

We will call our persona **Jen** and let's say we are a company that sells lawn services. Ask your team the following questions in order to create Jen:

1. How old is Jen?

2. Where does Jen live?

3. Does Jen have a family she lives with?

4. If she does have a family, who is in that family and what are their ages?

5. What type of job does Jen have?

6. Does Jen buy things online?

7. When does Jen buy things online?

8. Where does Jen get her news?

9. What is Jen interested in?

10. What kind of outside resources does Jen need to utilize for help at home?

Ok, let's start building our persona. Remember, this is our perfect customer we are trying to bring to life to discover her online habits in order to make our social media efforts successful. We will answer the questions now –

1) Jen is about 39 years old. She is active, plays tennis on the weekends and likes to go on hikes near where she lives.

2) Jen lives in a single-family home with 3 bedrooms and a garage and outdoor deck. Her home is in a neighborhood with about 50 other houses. In general the homes in her neighborhood are well cared for and most people have shrubs, potted flowers and lawns to mow.

3) Jen does have a family keeping her very busy, limiting her time to spend on household activities above and beyond the everyday things that need to be done.

4) Jen has a husband, Jim who works 40+ hours a week and a son, Dan who she shuffles to sporting practices 4 nights a week. Her son is 10 years old. Jen will be thinking about saving money for his college soon. Jen's husband is a sports enthusiast and that doesn't leave him much time after work to do things around the house. He prefers to hire someone else to do things like lawn care and house repairs.

5) Jen works in an office. She has been working there for 8 years and at lunchtime she eats with co-workers and goes online on her iPad to shop and look up sites the co-workers are talking about.

6) Jen finds shopping online very convenient. She would rather find goods and services online than anywhere else. She trusts sites like Yelp for business reviews, regularly checks her email and keeps up with trends on Pinterest and Twitter. She has a LinkedIn profile and a Facebook account.

7) Jen goes on line during her work breaks and after dinner at home. Friday nights and Sunday mornings she is also checking her social media sites, shopping online and preparing for the week ahead for things like school events, food prep for dinners and lunches, seasonal changes and where to get her car windshield repaired. She is solving household problems online.

8) Jen keeps up with family using Facebook and also uses Twitter to find her nightly news. She goes on local store sites to see if they are having clearance sales or special deals.

9) We know Jen likes tennis and keeping fit. She gets most of her friendships from people at work whom she eats lunch with and goes online with comparing deals, vacation plans and the latest style trends. She also likes collecting vintage pottery.

10) Jen works full time and takes care of her son. She generally makes the meals and pays the bills. She needs help cleaning the house, taking care of the lawn, uses a grocery delivery service and home maintenance services. Right now their furnace needs to be cleaned and the lawn is getting tall. There are hedges to be cut and weeding that needs to be done.

From this persona of Jen we know that a lawn service would be of help to her. So how do you find Jen on social media?

We know she uses Facebook, Pinterest and Twitter so those would be good places to start. We need content that she may be interested in reading. We also know that having a few good reviews on sites like Yelp will help get the lawn service business discovered.

SETTING UP GOALS

Create goals that are measurable and specific. Set time limits and be realistic about your goals. An example of a measurable goal is traffic to your website, finding out how long visitors stay on your site, know the bounce rate, track where your traffic is coming from.

After you set your goals, make an editorial calendar. List each social media site you plan on using.

Set up each day of the week with –

1. How many posts to plan
2. What type of content
3. Where your source content will come from –newsletters, trending posts, industry journals
4. When you plan to share your posts
5. Which analytics you need to measure sharing results

Quick Terms To Know

Bounce Rate – the amount of time visitors spend on your site
Bots – web spiders that crawl web content to index it
Index – search engines catalog web content for users to find
Pages Views – visits to a web page
Pingbacks – text that is trackable back to an original site
SERP – Search Engine Results Page (what you see after goggle a topic)
Sitelinks – additional subpage links for a specific site
Unique Visitors – first time visitors to your site

SECTION 2 SOCIAL MEDIA PLATFORMS

Let's Talk About Specific Social Media Platforms

Twitter

Twitter is the 140 characters count micro blogging service, which is used worldwide by over 310 million people, according to Google. People use hashtags (#) to look up information. If you plan on using Twitter, you should dedicate to tweeting at least 3 tweets a day. What should you tweet? Successful Twitter accounts in general do not use it solely to promote products/services. Your tweets should be a combination of useful information that viewers will want to share. Attached to your tweets should be your company information so viewers can reach you if they so desire. You can also use your Twitter to keep up with your competition and industry trends. Promoting good customer relationships with Twitter will help you address any issues fast and to a large audience if you have a lot of followers. A good daily Twitter practice is to review who followed you retweeted you and liked your tweets. Don't bother sending dm's (direct messages) to them, instead reward them with a re-tweet of their posts, like their posts or follow them if they fit your Twitter profile. Keep tract of your Twitter analytics with Twitters own free analytic tools. This is a quick way to review when your best tweet time is, what days are you getting the most attention and which tweets are the most popular.

Twitter analytics will also tell you whom you are attracting to your Twitter account. Is Jen one of your followers? If not, maybe you need to change your post material. Make sure you use hashtags on keywords to attract followers who fit your persona. For example, a lawn care business could tweet gardening tips or how to build your own fire pit, Jen might be interested in that.

Pinterest

Statistics by the marketresearch.com indicate that Pinterest has over 100 million active users as of 2015, about 85% are female. Remember Jen? We know she is one of those users. Should your lawn care business have a Pinterest profile? Most definitely! If you're not familiar with Pinterest, it is a system of electronic bulletin boards. You can have one board or as many as you like. You virtually pin posts to a board. The more pins you have, the better chance of someone re-pinning your pin to their board. This gets your business name and purpose out to your target audience. Again, careful crafting of your business Pinterest account is a must in order to attract your perfect persona as followers. It is easier to promote products and services on your own boards but a good Pinterest account will have a blend of useful information, interesting photos and tips, and subject matter that appeals to your persona. For example, our lawn care company may want to create a board with tennis tips and place it next to your lawn care Spring tips board.

An advantage with Pinterest is you do not have to pin everyday. A good practice is to set aside time once a week to add new pins to your boards. Unlike Twitter, Pinterest is not affected by a timeline so you do not need to dedicate specific times to pin.

Be sure to get credit for your pins by tagging them so when repined your company website information is seen and you can earn backlinks to your site. To attract followers, use catchy titles and titles that make clear what your board is about. Attractive, clear and colorful photos of the best quality get more repins.

Like Twitter, Pinterest has its own free analytic tool to use. To get the most out of your time pinning, view the analytics on a weekly basis to see what your most popular pins are, what is being repined and see the demographics of your pinners. Are you getting your persona Jen types following you? Be sure to check.

If your lucky, you may get a pin that goes viral, seen by millions of viewers!

Snapchat

This is a relatively new social media site but fast becoming the go to site for many. It is estimated that (mediakix.com) Snapchat gets 10 billion daily video views. It is in the top 3 for most downloaded apps in the United States and 70% of Snapchat users are women. Retailers are using Snapchat to send previews of new products, short video stories and giveaways to attract followers. A Snapchat is a 15 second video that disappears after it's viewed. The advantage to Snapchat is you can post your video anytime and its not effected by timelines. Your video will stay on your followers account until they have time to view it, then it will disappear after they have viewed it.

Whether you use Snapchat to give coupons, promote contests or giveaways, plan your business strategy on your editorial calendar to keep your message on point and blended with other social media sites you use.

Instagram

According to Instagram, they have over 400 million users worldwide. It can be used as an influencer-marketing tool. Celebrities get on Instagram using a product and voila! Instant success! Instagram is particularly useful for certain types of businesses such as the beauty industry. Highly polished photos of rich imagery help build followings. An advantage of Instagram is that it is easy for mobile users. You can upload photos on your smartphone and apply various filters instantly. You can cross promote your Instagram feed on other social media sites like Facebook. Find influencers on Instagram by leveraging lists through Google. Be specific on your search terms. Instead of searching "top landscapers" do "top landscapers in the northwest", then follow the influencers in your industry. Keep a uniform consistent look to your Instagram feed. Plan your message and post high quality photos or videos. Use hashtags in your descriptions and as with any social media site, always look at the stats. It is the only way you will know if your efforts are moving the business brand in the right direction.

Tumblr

Tumblr has over 23.2 million users in the United States according to E-Marketer. Most of the users are between 25 to 34 years of age. Out of those users, 78% are accessing Tumblr through a mobile device. Tumblr is available in 16 languages. The advantage of using Tumblr is you can post videos and multiple types of media intermixed. This micro blogging platform makes it easy to do that without much technical knowledge. Measure your stats by installing a free statcounter which will keep track of your visitors, hits and website stats.

Vine

Vine is a video platform that you can take a 6 second video on your smartphone and quickly post it to your Vine account. Because Vine videos are only 6 seconds long, you must be creative. An advantage of using Vine is you can loop the videos and easily share on your Twitter or Facebook timelines. Vines are meant to be fun videos showing something an audience will want to see. Today, people use Vine in hopes that they will produce a viral Vine video thus getting their brand seen by millions of viewers. Hashtags will increase your effectiveness. Vine is most popular in the United States followed by the UK and Mexico. You can see on your Vine account how many times your video has been played.

YouTube

YouTube is also a video site but unlike Vine, it has no time limits. You must create a YouTube channel in order to post your videos. To create a YouTube channel first open an account with a Gmail address. If you do not have Gmail, make a Gmail account because everything is linked with Google. Be sure to keep your branding in mind and title your email with the name you plan on giving your channel. This name should also match all your social media sites, like Twitter and Facebook. You need to use a computer to make your channel.

Click on your profile gravatar and you will see a Creator Studio and a gear. Click the gear to get the Create a Channel and boom; you just created your YouTube channel. There are many
YouTube videos to watch on how to make videos, equipment you may need and how to run a successful channel. If you have the time, a good short video, less than 5 minutes that has great content will be an asset to your social media marketing strategy.

Facebook

Most everyone knows what Facebook is but using Facebook for business is a little different than personal use. First thing you need to do is set up a Facebook Business Page. If your business does not have a Facebook account, make an account. Click the arrow in right hand corner, choose Create Page. Choose a business category for your page. Next choose your industry category and add a profile picture, business name, info and click Save. You are automatically set up as the administrator for the page. To add someone else, go to Manage Page in Settings menu.

Your page is where you can add photos, list details like hours you are open and post updates about promotions and sales. Customers can leave feedback and write reviews about your business. Encourage viewers to use social share buttons when they visit your page. This makes it easy for viewers to share your content. Add links to your website and social media sites. You can easily add posts by clicking the post button. You can also create Facebook Ads, click on Ad Creation, choose your business objective; this is a paid service though, not free! You can manage multiple ads in the Ads Manager and edit your ad. Your Facebook Business Page is a great place to run promotions and contests. Be sure to mention your Facebook Page on your YouTube channel.

Google+

A lot can be said about Google. According to Wikipedia Google indexes billions of web pages and is the dominant search engine in the United States. Google, with over 400 million users, is an important part of your site for search engine ranking. The first thing you should do is fill out your Google profile completely. Next add Google Maps to your website and create a Google sitemap to make your site more searchable for the search bots. Google has in-depth analytics tool, keyword planner and extensive tutorials on how to use their tools. Google Apps can bring your on line office together with Gmail, Google Docs, your YouTube channel, calendars, videos and photos just to mention a few important resources.

LinkedIn

This is a valuable site for business people. It is not a place to sell your wares. Use LinkedIn to build professional relationships. It takes only a few minutes to set up your profile and is not a site that you need to interact on daily or even weekly basis so it is easy to maintain. Use LinkedIn to find other like-minded business people, join groups and keep on top of your industry trends. Joining a group and becoming a contributor is a fast way to gain access to a large group of people if it has many members. If you see a need that is not covered, start your own group; encourage members to contribute content, use it to establish yourself as an expert in your industry. Find business opportunities, build up your business contacts and increase your networking possibilities on LinkedIn.

So there you have it, the top big 10 social media sites, which one should you choose? Let's see . . .

A good place to start is by choosing 2 sites to concentrate on. Keeping up with posts and engagement on 2 major sites can be overwhelming when you first start.

Lets go back to our persona Jen. From what we have learned about Jen, I would pick Pinterest and Twitter as my two main sites. This is a good blend because Pinterest does not need to be maintained on a daily basis but Twitter does need engagement everyday in order to become successful.

To begin, start by making a goal lists with simple goals like how many followers a month do you want to attract? What type of engagement rate are you looking for?

Set up your editorial calendar, even if it's just yourself running the show, a calendar will be your social media roadmap and will keep you driving in the right direction.

Other Social Media Sites To Consider

Social Media Search & Review Sites

Another valuable asset to your social media strategy is a social media search & reviews site. These are sites that you don't need to maintain but do need to respond to if a customer writes a bad review of your business. There are local search sites as well as business specific search sites for example you can search for restaurants on zomato.com or tripadvisor.com. You may have heard of some of these sites such as Yelp. Yelp is a site that lists businesses and people can write a review of a business and give it a star rating. This may sound scary but it is a very useful tool in promoting your business on social media.

To get your business on Yelp, first make an account with Yelp. Next, click the "claim your business" button to set up your Yelp Business Page. You can also search for your business name on biz.yelp.com. Add photos, menus and offers to your page. On the Yelp site there are tips for businesses and how to communicate with customers.

Other online search sites to join include:

Expedia	Yelp
Kayak	Greenpal
Magic Yellow	Zomato
Insiderpages	Zagat
Citysquares	Urbanspoon
Tripadvisor	Bing
Foursquare	Yahoo
Cityslick.Net	Thumbtack
Manta	Home Advisor
Local.Com	Restaurants.Com
Whitepages	Google
Angie's list	
Yellowbook	
Mapquest	

Plus many, many more are out there. Search your local area for popular sites to list your business on.

Another good SEO practice for your social media strategy is to be listed on search engine sites like Google and Bing. They both have business-listing pages and give detailed analytics on how many visits, clicks, followers and actions on your posts. To start just make an account and follow the site instructions.

SECTION 3 LET'S TALK ABOUT YOUR WEBSITE . . .

Today anyone can make a simple website with templates offered by various companies but many of those sites will not be indexed by search engines and therefore will not come up when viewers are searching for that product or service. If you don't have a website, WordPress.com is a good place to start for a free, easy to build first site. WordPress has many great tutorials to help the beginner.

So How Do You Make Your Site Come Up In Searches?

Keywords

Keywords are what the search bots look for to identify and index content on the web. If you do not have keywords in titles and content, your chances of search bots or spiders finding your site goes down dramatically. I see many businesses title their site with a name that has no association with the service they are providing. For example, if your selling children's clothing and title your site "Ally By the Sea" no one will know what you do. If for some reason you like that name or it has meaning to you, a more appropriate title might be "Ally's Kids Clothing by the Sea". With keywords in your title, the little spiders will get that you sell children's clothing.

There are many free tools you can use to find keywords. Google has the most popular keyword finder, which is Google Keyword Tool. You can identify and optimize your site to improve search ranking, track competitors sites and find out what search terms their customers are using. Google Insights is another tool, which searches geographical areas and the search volume in those areas for keywords.

You should have a sprinkling of keywords throughout your site. A good place to start making sure you have keywords is in any links on pages to forms that viewers will be filling out. But be careful, those search bots are sensitive to over stacking keywords for higher search rankings and you can be penalized by search engines.

Link Building

What Is Link Building?

Link building is a multi faceted process of having healthy links on web pages, which point back to your site. These links are analyzed by search bots to determine if the source is trustworthy and if the information is of importance.

How Do You Build Links?

The easiest place to start is on your website. Be sure to add social sharing buttons on every page and posts. Social share buttons are link buttons viewers click on to share your content on Twitter, Facebook, Pinterest, Tumblr and any other social media site that you add a button for.

Another thing to add to your website is your social media feeds, but only if you are actively using them such as your Twitter feed. But be aware, sometimes feeds can slow down mobile page load time, which will make you loose some mobile traffic if your site is to slow to download.

Blog Content - Does Your Site Have A Blog?

Blogging is a great way to get useful content out on the web. If you do start a blog on your site, take time to keep fresh content on it. Don't let too much time go by in between posts. If you find your time is limited, repurpose your most popular posts. To do this, check your blog analytics to find the most popular posts and update any facts, check any links to make sure they still work and give your post a current date, and voila! You have repurposed good content. Good content is always good content!

Looking for content for your blog?

Interviews are a way of establishing relationships. Post your interview on your site and chances are that interviewee will link back to your site.

Tutorials are always popular. Viewers go on-line to find out "how to" do anything and everything today.

Keep up with industry trends. There are always improvements and trends in any field, blog about those trends first and be the blog to read in your line of business.

Infographics, new online apps or tools and guides are useful content that viewers like to share on their social media sites because they are colorful, fast to read and have useful content.

SEO

Why Is This Important?

SEO is search engine optimization

Like keywords, SEO is how search engines find your site and index your content for viewers. If your site is not coming up on the first or second search page results or SERP, you will not get many visitors to your site. Here are some SEO tips to follow. .

1. Start by submitting your site to Google to be indexed. Make sure your site has a Google Sitemap. This will relate the structure of your site's web pages into an easily readable map for the bots.

2. If you have a WordPress site, installing a SEO plugin like Yoast will help you optimize your site for SEO.

3. Images are a big deal if they are not optimized for the web. Make sure your images have their descriptions and alt text filled in. Be sure to use proper tags, check your image load times and format on a mobile device. Be aware of the size requirement for the social media platforms you are posting to.

4. Set up Google Analytics for your site to measure your ROI and track your social media networking sites.

5. Check your site for bad links and fix them. Search bots do not like links that are broken.

6. Set up 301 redirects for any 404-page errors, which are Page Not Found errors.

7. Make sure your keywords are still relevant in current searches for your industry.

8. Canonicalization is an important word. If a search engine comes across a site that appears to have more than 1 URL, it will not be able to determine which URL to use to index that site which will result in the site not appearing in SERP results. For example:

http:// sitename.com vs. http:// www. sitename.com may be the same site but a search engine will not know how to rank this site.

JUST A QUICK NOTE ABOUT JPEGS, GIFS AND PNGS

– What Is The Difference Between These Types of Images For Web Pages?

jpeg – this is a format for photographs, it makes it easier to resize photos without losing quality if they are saved as a jpeg.

gif – this is used for graphics. Your logo for example might be saved as a gif. Gifs are commonly used in animation. Another important feature of a gif is it can have a transparent background.

png – can be used for photos and graphics, has a higher compression than gifs and jpegs. Pngs support higher levels of transparency in computer art.

Landing Page

Do You Have A "Landing Page"?

A landing page is a call-to-action form you want your viewers to complete. This is not your home page. Landing pages need to be designed with little distraction and only one clickable link, the Call To Action item.

A good landing page has 3 parts –
- ✓ **Start Action**
- ✓ **Action**
- ✓ **Result**

Start Action

When designing your landing page you need to ask this question – what do I want my visitor to do?

- ➤ SUBSCRIBE TO MY NEWSLETTER?
- ➤ MAKE AN APPOINTMENT?
- ➤ WATCH A DEMO VIDEO?
- ➤ RECEIVE MY E-BOOK?

After you answer that question, this becomes your goal. You should have only one goal on a landing page. More than one goal will make it difficult for a viewer to make a decision and you may loose them. Your page should be simple, clear and concise.

Leave off the footer and navigation bar. Do not have any clickable links that you may have on your website, like a logo. The only clickable link should be your Call To Action.

Action

Your visitor has actually landed on your landing page. Now what?

You need a headline that grabs a visitor's attention. Use keywords that your visitor used to find you. A good practice is to run your headline through a headline analyzer.

Keep your copy simple and compelling to keep your viewer interested. Not easy to do, but if you can get your message across to the viewer about how this product or service will help them solve their problem, you've done your job!

Next comes your Call-To-Action button or **CTA**. Have an actionable sentence with words like "how to" or "find out" to compel the viewer to click that button.

Now that you have gotten the visitor this far, don't stop now.

Result

Go further than a simple "thank you for signing up" email. Let them know how valuable their time is; make them feel good about giving you their email address. The after email can be a more in-depth conversation, more personal like asking a question or telling them a little more about the newsletter or e-book they signed up for. Make sure your visitors get immediate access to what they signed up for.

SECTION 4   CONCLUSION

We started out by developing our target audience persona "Jen", discovered where she is on-line.

1. LOOKED AT THE TOP 10 BIG SOCIAL MEDIA SITES

2. DISCOVERED REVIEW SITES

3. TALKED ABOUT YOUR WEBSITE

> KEYWORDS
> LINK BUILDING
> BLOG CONTENT
> SEO
> LANDING PAGES

Your social media strategy is off to a good start!   Follow these checklist items and you will soon have a successful social media following!

✓ KNOW YOUR AUDIENCE
Develop your target audience by making a marketing "persona". This will help you narrow your decision making process of which social media platforms you should be on and you will be better able to tailor your marketing message to potential customers.

✓ HAVE GOALS
Create goals that are specific and measurable. Set time limits to meet your goals and be realistic about them.

✓ HAVE A PLAN

Make an editorial calendar with all your social media platforms, times to post, types of posts, who is in charge of the post and analyze the performance of the post.

✓ ENGAGE YOUR AUDIENCE

Develop good quality content that viewers will want to share. Content that solves a problem or creates solutions makes good sharable content. Have a landing page with a sign up for your newsletter or e-book. Be sure to go the extra mile on your "thank you" email by being personal; expand on the nature of your giveaway.

✓ ANALIZE YOUR STATS

Can't say how important this is. Statistics are of no value if you don't pay attention to them. Measure conversion rate, traffic sources, and number of visitors and in-bound links. This is the only way to find out if you are "on message" and reaching your target audience.

✓ BE CONSISTANT

Stay on point to what you post and share. You have developed your audience; keep sharing useful content with them.

✓ RE-PURPOSE GOOD CONTENT

Remember your stats? Find out which posts performed the best and re-post. Update an old post by doing a fact check and make sure all links still work. Good content is still good content and useful information never goes out of style.

✓ SHARE ON SOCIAL MEDIA

Make sure you participate on social media. Do some sharing yourself, comment on others blogs, like a Facebook Page, re-tweet and share other people's useful content.

GOOD LUCK WITH YOUR SOCIAL MEDIA STRATEGY!

SHARE THIS BOOK

If this book has inspired you to start your social media strategy, please share on Facebook, Twitter, Pinterest, Instagram and any other social media site you use. You can also review this book on Amazon.

Please visit my website and share your story on how social media has benefitted your business. Go to:

www.successfulsocialmedia.net

ABOUT

Roberta Alluzio is an entrepreneur, online marketer, blogger, and photographer. Her passion is to help other entrepreneurs worldwide become successful online through social media marketing.

Visit Roberta on Twitter @RobertaCodes

ACKNOWLEDGMENTS

I would like to thank my family for their love and support. I would also like to thank all the wonderful people who have given me inspiration in writing this book and encourage everyone out there to follow your dreams, do what you love and love what you do.

www.ingramcontent.com/pod-product-compliance
Lightning Source LLC
Chambersburg PA
CBHW071834200526
45169CB00018B/1498